# Highly Effective Habits!

Laurel D. Malvern

Copyright & Legal Disclaimer:

Copyright © 2024 by Laurel D. Malvern

All rights reserved. No part of this publication may be reproduced, distributed, or transmitted in any form or by any means, including photocopying, recording, or other electronic or mechanical methods, without the prior written permission of the publisher, except in the case of brief quotations embodied in critical reviews and certain other noncommercial uses permitted by copyright law.

The information provided in this book, "Highly Effective Habits," is for educational and informational purposes only. The author, Laurel D. Malvern, and the publisher make no representations or warranties with respect to the accuracy, applicability, or completeness of the contents of this book. They disclaim any responsibility for any loss or damages resulting from the use of information contained herein.

The topics covered in this book, including success, business culture, self-help, management, motivation and leadership, personal finance, processes, and infrastructure, are intended to provide readers with a comprehensive understanding of the subject matter. However, individual circumstances may vary, and readers are encouraged to seek professional advice or assistance when necessary.

The strategies, techniques, and suggestions presented in this book are based on the author's experiences and research. Results may vary, and success is not guaranteed. The author and publisher shall not be liable for any direct, indirect, incidental, consequential, or punitive damages arising out of the use of this book.

Reading and implementing the concepts and practices outlined in "Highly Effective Habits" are done so at the reader's own discretion and risk. The author and publisher shall not be held responsible for any adverse effects or consequences resulting from the application of the information provided.

By reading this book, the reader agrees to indemnify and hold harmless the author, Laurel D. Malvern, and the publisher from any claims, damages, losses, or liabilities arising from the reader's use of or reliance on the information contained herein.

Any references to third-party products, services, or organizations are provided for informational purposes only and do not constitute endorsement or recommendation. The author and publisher disclaim any responsibility for the content or actions of third parties.

By accessing and reading "Highly Effective Habits," the reader acknowledges and agrees to abide by the terms of this copyright and legal disclaimer.

For permissions requests or inquiries, please contact the publisher at the address provided in the book.

"Highly Effective Habits"

Chapter Introduction: The Power of Highly Effective Habits 7

Chapter: Unveiling the Power of Highly Effective Habits 8

Chapter: Unveiling the Purpose 9

Chapter: Understanding Success 11

Chapter: The Power of Clear Goals and Aligned Values 13

Chapter: The Role of Effective Habits in Sustainable Success 15

Chapter: Building a Thriving Business Culture 17

Chapter: Harnessing Habits to Shape Organizational Culture 20

Chapter: Case Studies of Exceptional Organizational Cultures 23

Chapter: Empowering Self-Help Strategies for Personal Growth 26

Chapter: Cultivating Personal Excellence Through Mindfulness, Self-Reflection, and Continuous Learning 28

Chapter: Actionable Tips for Daily Habits that Enhance Well-Being and Fulfillment 30

Chapter: The Habits of Highly Effective Managers and Leaders 33

Chapter: The Crucial Trio: Communication, Delegation, and Decision-Making in Leadership 36

Chapter: Case Studies of Successful Leaders Demonstrating Effective Communication, Delegation, and Decision-Making 38

Chapter: Unleashing the Power of Motivation and Inspiration 41

Chapter: Strategies for Sustaining Motivation and Overcoming Obstacles 43

Chapter: The Transformative Power of Positive Thinking and Motivated Habits 46

Chapter: Mastering Personal Finance: Habits for Financial Success and Stability 49

Chapter: Building Financial Wellness: Budgeting, Saving, Investing, and Debt Management 52

Chapter: Practical Steps for Developing Healthy Financial Habits and Achieving Long-Term Goals 55

Chapter: Streamlining Processes and Infrastructure: Enhancing Efficiency in Business and Life 58

Chapter: Mastering Time Management, Organization, and Prioritization Habits 61

Chapter: Strategies for Streamlining Processes and Improving Infrastructure 65

Conclusion: Cultivating Highly Effective Habits for Success 68

Chapter: Take Action: Committing to Highly Effective Habits 70

Chapter: Transformative Change: Achieving Lasting Success through Effective Habits 73

# Chapter Introduction: The Power of Highly Effective Habits

Welcome to the world of highly effective habits, where small actions lead to significant results and success becomes a way of life. In this chapter, we embark on a journey to explore the profound impact that habits have on our ability to achieve success in every area of our lives. From personal growth to professional advancement, the habits we cultivate shape our behaviors, attitudes, and outcomes. Join me as we delve into the essence of highly effective habits and uncover the key to unlocking your full potential.

# Chapter: Unveiling the Power of Highly Effective Habits

In the pursuit of success, we often seek grand gestures and monumental breakthroughs, overlooking the transformative potential of daily habits. Yet, it is these seemingly mundane routines that wield the greatest influence over our lives. Welcome to the realm of highly effective habits, where the small, consistent actions we take pave the path to extraordinary achievements.

In this chapter, we embark on a journey to uncover the significance of highly effective habits in achieving success across all facets of life. From personal growth and professional advancement to financial prosperity and fulfillment, the habits we cultivate serve as the cornerstone of our journey toward excellence.

As we delve deeper into the concept of highly effective habits, we'll explore their profound impact on shaping our behaviors, attitudes, and outcomes. Through real-life examples and compelling insights, we'll witness firsthand the transformative power of intentional habits in creating the life we desire.

Join me as we unlock the secrets to success by harnessing the power of highly effective habits. Together, we'll embark on a journey of self-discovery and growth, where every small action brings us closer to realizing our dreams and aspirations.

# Chapter: Unveiling the Purpose

As you hold this book in your hands, you may wonder: What sets "Highly Effective Habits" apart from the myriad of self-help guides promising transformative change? The answer lies in its core purpose: to empower you with practical insights and strategies to cultivate highly effective habits that will propel you towards success in every facet of life.

The purpose of this book is not merely to impart knowledge but to catalyze action. It serves as a guiding light, illuminating the path towards personal and professional growth, financial stability, and fulfillment. Through its pages, you will embark on a journey of self-discovery and empowerment, armed with the tools and techniques necessary to transform your life.

At its heart, "Highly Effective Habits" is a blueprint for success—a roadmap that navigates the complexities of modern life and charts a course towards excellence. It is a testament to the power of deliberate action and intentional living, showing you how small, consistent habits can yield remarkable results over time.

Through a blend of practical insights, real-life examples, and actionable strategies, this book equips you with the knowledge and tools needed to cultivate habits that will propel you towards your goals. Whether you aspire to climb the corporate ladder, build a thriving business, or simply lead a more fulfilling life, the principles outlined in these pages will guide you every step of the way.

So, as you embark on this journey, remember that the purpose of "Highly Effective Habits" extends beyond mere words on a page. It is a call to action—a call to embrace change, cultivate resilience, and unleash your full potential. May this book serve as a catalyst for transformation in your life, empowering you to become the architect of your own success.

# Chapter: Understanding Success

Success—a word often spoken, yet its definition remains elusive, subjective, and deeply personal. In this chapter, we embark on a journey to unravel the multifaceted nature of success, exploring its various dimensions, including personal, professional, and financial.

At its core, success transcends mere achievement—it encompasses a holistic sense of fulfillment and accomplishment that resonates with our deepest aspirations. It is the realization of our dreams, the attainment of our goals, and the manifestation of our highest potential.

Personal Success: For many, personal success lies in the pursuit of happiness, fulfillment, and self-actualization. It is the journey of self-discovery, growth, and authenticity—the pursuit of living a life aligned with our values, passions, and purpose. Personal success may manifest in the form of meaningful relationships, inner peace, spiritual enlightenment, or simply a sense of contentment and well-being.

Professional Success: In the realm of career and professional endeavors, success often revolves around recognition, advancement, and mastery. It is the culmination of hard work, dedication, and skill—the attainment of goals, milestones, and accolades in one's chosen field. Professional success may manifest in the form of job satisfaction, career progression, leadership roles, or entrepreneurial achievements.

Financial Success: While not the sole measure of success, financial prosperity plays a significant role in our ability to lead fulfilling lives. It is the ability to manage resources wisely, generate wealth, and achieve financial independence—the freedom to pursue our passions, support our loved ones, and contribute to causes greater than ourselves. Financial success may manifest in the form of financial security, abundance, and the ability to live comfortably within one's means.

As we navigate the complexities of success, it is essential to recognize that success is not a destination but a journey—a continuous evolution of growth, learning, and adaptation. It is a dynamic process that requires resilience, perseverance, and a willingness to embrace change.

In the pages that follow, we will delve deeper into the principles and practices that underpin success, exploring how highly effective habits can serve as the building blocks for achieving success in every area of our lives. So, let us embark on this journey of exploration and discovery, as we seek to understand success and unlock its boundless potential.

# Chapter: The Power of Clear Goals and Aligned Values

In the pursuit of success, setting clear goals and aligning them with our values serves as the compass that guides our journey. In this chapter, we explore the profound importance of this fundamental principle, delving into how it shapes our actions, decisions, and ultimately, our destiny.

Setting Clear Goals: Goals are the milestones that mark our path towards success, providing direction, motivation, and focus. Clear goals serve as beacons of light in the darkness, illuminating the path ahead and guiding our actions towards desired outcomes. Whether they are short-term objectives or long-term aspirations, clear goals provide clarity of purpose and a roadmap for achievement.

When we set clear goals, we create a blueprint for success — a roadmap that outlines the steps needed to turn our dreams into reality. By breaking down our goals into manageable tasks and milestones, we can measure progress, stay on track, and course-correct when necessary. Clear goals empower us to prioritize our efforts, allocate resources wisely, and overcome obstacles with resilience and determination.

Aligning with Values: While goals provide direction, our values serve as the guiding principles that shape our journey. Our values are the core beliefs and principles that define who we are, what we stand for, and what matters most to us. When our goals align with our values, we experience a profound sense of purpose, meaning, and fulfillment.

Aligning our goals with our values ensures that our efforts are directed towards outcomes that resonate with our deepest aspirations and desires. It enables us to pursue success in a way that is authentic, meaningful, and aligned with our true selves. When our goals reflect our values, we are more likely to experience a sense of fulfillment and satisfaction, regardless of the outcome.

Moreover, aligning our goals with our values helps us make better decisions, navigate challenges, and stay true to ourselves in the face of adversity. It strengthens our resolve, enhances our resilience, and fosters a sense of integrity and authenticity in everything we do.

In essence, setting clear goals and aligning them with our values is not just about achieving success — it's about living a life of purpose, passion, and meaning. It is about pursuing our dreams with intention, integrity, and authenticity, and creating a life that reflects who we truly are and what we truly value.

# Chapter: The Role of Effective Habits in Sustainable Success

In the pursuit of success, our habits are the invisible threads that weave the fabric of our lives. In this chapter, we explore the pivotal role that effective habits play in not only attaining success but also sustaining it over time. Through their consistency and cumulative impact, effective habits become the driving force behind our achievements and the bedrock upon which lasting success is built.

Attaining Success: Effective habits serve as the cornerstone of success, providing the structure and discipline necessary to turn aspirations into reality. When we consistently engage in habits that align with our goals and values, we create the conditions for success to flourish. Whether it's waking up early to pursue personal development, dedicating time each day to honing our skills, or maintaining a healthy work-life balance, effective habits ensure that we make progress towards our goals with purpose and intention.

Sustaining Success: Yet, achieving success is not merely about reaching a destination—it's about maintaining momentum and staying the course in the face of challenges and setbacks. This is where the power of effective habits truly shines. By ingraining habits that promote resilience, adaptability, and continual improvement, we cultivate the mindset and behaviors necessary to navigate the ups and downs of the journey.

Effective habits provide us with the stability and consistency needed to weather storms and overcome obstacles with grace and determination. Whether it's maintaining a positive attitude in the face of adversity, seeking opportunities for growth and learning, or staying committed to our long-term vision, our habits serve as the anchor that keeps us grounded and focused on the path ahead.

Moreover, effective habits foster a sense of accountability and self-discipline that empowers us to stay true to our commitments and priorities. By establishing routines and rituals that support our goals, we create a framework for success that withstands the test of time. Whether it's carving out time each day for reflection and planning, or surrounding ourselves with like-minded individuals who inspire and motivate us, our habits shape the environment in which success thrives.

In essence, the role of effective habits in attaining and sustaining success cannot be overstated. They are the building blocks upon which our achievements are built, the fuel that propels us forward, and the compass that guides us towards our dreams. By cultivating habits that align with our goals and values, we unlock the power to create a life of purpose, passion, and fulfillment — one habit at a time.

# Chapter: Building a Thriving Business Culture

In the dynamic landscape of modern business, a thriving organizational culture is not just a desirable trait—it is a competitive advantage that drives innovation, fosters collaboration, and fuels growth. In this chapter, we delve into the essential elements of a positive and productive business culture, exploring how they contribute to creating an environment where individuals can thrive, teams can excel, and organizations can flourish.

Shared Vision and Values: At the heart of a thriving business culture lies a shared sense of purpose and values that unite individuals and align their efforts towards a common goal. A clear and compelling vision provides a sense of direction and inspires individuals to strive for excellence, while shared values serve as guiding principles that shape behaviors, decisions, and interactions within the organization.

Open Communication and Transparency: Effective communication is the lifeblood of any successful organization, fostering trust, collaboration, and engagement among team members. A culture of open communication and transparency encourages dialogue, feedback, and idea-sharing at all levels of the organization, empowering individuals to voice their opinions, express their concerns, and contribute to the collective success of the team.

Empowerment and Accountability: In a thriving business culture, individuals are empowered to take ownership of their work, make decisions, and drive meaningful change. Leaders delegate authority and responsibility, trusting employees to take initiative and innovate, while holding them accountable for results. By fostering a culture of empowerment and accountability, organizations cultivate a sense of ownership and pride among their team members, leading to increased motivation, productivity, and performance.

Continuous Learning and Development: A commitment to lifelong learning and professional development is a hallmark of a thriving business culture. Organizations that prioritize training, mentorship, and growth opportunities for their employees create an environment where individuals can develop their skills, expand their knowledge, and unlock their full potential. By investing in the growth and development of their workforce, organizations not only enhance employee engagement and retention but also strengthen their competitive position in the marketplace.

Diversity and Inclusion: In today's globalized world, diversity and inclusion are essential components of a thriving business culture. Embracing diversity of thought, background, and perspective fosters creativity, innovation, and resilience within organizations, enabling them to adapt to changing market dynamics and seize new opportunities. By creating a culture of inclusivity where all individuals feel valued, respected, and empowered to contribute, organizations can leverage the unique strengths and talents of their diverse workforce to drive sustainable growth and success.

In summary, building a thriving business culture requires a concerted effort to nurture shared vision and values, foster open communication and transparency, empower individuals, and hold them accountable, prioritize continuous learning and development, and embrace diversity and inclusion. By cultivating a positive and productive culture, organizations can create an environment where individuals can thrive, teams can excel, and business can flourish in today's ever-evolving marketplace.

# Chapter: Harnessing Habits to Shape Organizational Culture

In the intricate ecosystem of organizational culture, habits serve as the invisible threads that weave together the fabric of beliefs, behaviors, and norms within an organization. In this chapter, we explore the profound impact that habits have on shaping organizational culture and fostering employee engagement and satisfaction.

Cultural Norms and Rituals: Habits form the backbone of cultural norms and rituals within organizations, shaping the way work is done and interactions are conducted on a daily basis. From morning stand-up meetings to end-of-week celebrations, these habitual routines create a sense of continuity and belonging among employees, reinforcing shared values, and fostering a cohesive organizational culture.

Communication and Collaboration: Habits play a crucial role in shaping communication and collaboration patterns within organizations, influencing how information flows, decisions are made, and ideas are shared. Whether it's the habit of actively listening during meetings, providing timely feedback, or collaborating across teams, these habits promote transparency, trust, and teamwork, enhancing employee engagement and satisfaction.

Leadership Behaviors: The habits exhibited by leaders within an organization have a ripple effect that permeates through the entire culture. Leaders who model habits of integrity, empathy, and accountability set the tone for a positive and inclusive organizational culture, inspiring trust, and confidence among employees. By leading by example and consistently demonstrating behaviors that align with organizational values, leaders can cultivate a culture of excellence and engagement that drives employee satisfaction and performance.

Recognition and Reward Systems: Habits also influence the way recognition and reward systems are implemented within organizations, shaping employee motivation and morale. Whether it's the habit of acknowledging and celebrating individual and team achievements, or the habit of providing constructive feedback and coaching, these practices reinforce desired behaviors and performance standards, fostering a culture of appreciation and recognition that enhances employee engagement and satisfaction.

Work-Life Balance: In today's fast-paced work environment, habits related to work-life balance are becoming increasingly important in shaping organizational culture and employee well-being. Organizations that prioritize habits such as setting boundaries, promoting flexibility, and encouraging self-care create an environment where employees feel supported, valued, and empowered to achieve a healthy balance between their personal and professional lives. By fostering a culture that values and prioritizes employee well-being, organizations can enhance employee satisfaction, retention, and productivity.

In conclusion, habits play a pivotal role in shaping organizational culture and fostering employee engagement and satisfaction. By cultivating habits that promote communication, collaboration, leadership, recognition, work-life balance, and other positive behaviors, organizations can create a culture that empowers employees to thrive, innovate, and contribute to the collective success of the organization.

# Chapter: Case Studies of Exceptional Organizational Cultures

In the realm of business, certain companies stand out not only for their financial success but also for their exceptional organizational cultures. In this chapter, we examine several renowned companies known for their strong organizational cultures and the habits they cultivate to foster employee engagement, satisfaction, and overall success.

Google: Renowned for its innovative and dynamic workplace culture, Google has cultivated a set of habits that prioritize creativity, collaboration, and employee well-being. Among these habits are the famous "20% time" policy, which encourages employees to spend a portion of their workweek pursuing passion projects, fostering a culture of innovation and experimentation. Additionally, Google's emphasis on data-driven decision-making and transparent communication ensures that employees feel empowered to contribute their ideas and opinions, driving continuous improvement and innovation across the organization.

Zappos: Known for its legendary customer service and vibrant company culture, Zappos has built its success on a foundation of core values and habits that prioritize employee happiness and satisfaction. One of the most notable habits cultivated at Zappos is the emphasis on company culture fit during the hiring process, ensuring that new hires align with the organization's values and contribute positively to its culture. Additionally, Zappos encourages a spirit of autonomy and creativity among its employees, empowering them to take ownership of their work and make decisions that prioritize customer satisfaction above all else.

Netflix: As a pioneer in the streaming entertainment industry, Netflix has garnered attention not only for its innovative business model but also for its unique organizational culture. Central to Netflix's culture is the concept of "freedom and responsibility," which empowers employees to take ownership of their work and make decisions autonomously. Netflix also cultivates a culture of feedback and continuous improvement, with regular "360-degree" performance reviews that encourage open, honest communication and accountability at all levels of the organization.

Southwest Airlines: With its legendary commitment to customer service and employee engagement, Southwest Airlines has established itself as a leader in the airline industry. At the heart of Southwest's culture is a set of core values, including a "Warrior Spirit," a "Servant's Heart," and a "Fun-LUVing Attitude," which guide employees' actions and behaviors. Southwest also cultivates a habit of servant leadership, with leaders at all levels of the organization prioritizing the needs of their teams and leading by example with humility, integrity, and empathy.

In conclusion, these companies serve as shining examples of the transformative power of strong organizational cultures and the habits they cultivate. By prioritizing values such as innovation, collaboration, autonomy, and customer service, these companies have not only achieved financial success but have also created environments where employees feel empowered, engaged, and inspired to achieve their full potential.

# Chapter: Empowering Self-Help Strategies for Personal Growth

In the pursuit of personal growth and development, self-help strategies serve as invaluable tools for individuals seeking to unlock their full potential and live a life of purpose, passion, and fulfillment. In this chapter, we introduce readers to essential self-help practices that can catalyze transformation and empower them to embark on a journey of self-discovery and growth.

Mindfulness and Meditation: At the core of personal growth lies the practice of mindfulness and meditation, which involve cultivating present-moment awareness and fostering a deep connection with oneself. By engaging in regular mindfulness and meditation practices, individuals can develop greater clarity, resilience, and emotional intelligence, enabling them to navigate life's challenges with grace and equanimity.

Self-Reflection and Journaling: Self-reflection and journaling are powerful tools for gaining insight into one's thoughts, feelings, and behaviors, and fostering self-awareness. By setting aside time for introspection and writing down their thoughts and experiences, individuals can gain clarity on their values, goals, and priorities, and identify areas for growth and improvement.

Goal Setting and Action Planning: Setting clear, achievable goals is essential for personal growth, as it provides direction and motivation to pursue one's aspirations. By defining specific, measurable goals and creating action plans to achieve them, individuals can take concrete steps towards realizing their dreams and aspirations, and track their progress along the way.

Continuous Learning and Skill Development: Lifelong learning and skill development are foundational to personal growth, as they enable individuals to expand their knowledge, acquire new skills, and adapt to changing circumstances. Whether through formal education, self-study, or experiential learning, individuals can continually challenge themselves to grow and evolve, unlocking new opportunities for personal and professional advancement.

Positive Affirmations and Visualization: Positive affirmations and visualization techniques are powerful tools for cultivating a positive mindset and manifesting one's desires. By repeating affirmations that affirm their worthiness, capabilities, and potential, individuals can reprogram their subconscious mind and overcome self-limiting beliefs. Likewise, visualization techniques enable individuals to mentally rehearse their desired outcomes, enhancing confidence, motivation, and resilience in the face of challenges.

In summary, self-help strategies are essential for personal growth and development, providing individuals with the tools and techniques needed to cultivate self-awareness, set goals, take action, and manifest their desires. By incorporating these practices into their daily lives, individuals can embark on a journey of self-discovery and transformation, unlocking their full potential and living a life of purpose, passion, and fulfillment.

# Chapter: Cultivating Personal Excellence Through Mindfulness, Self-Reflection, and Continuous Learning

In the pursuit of personal excellence, certain foundational practices serve as pillars upon which individuals can build a life of purpose, fulfillment, and growth. In this chapter, we explore three essential topics—mindfulness, self-reflection, and continuous learning—and how they contribute to personal development and lifelong success.

Mindfulness: Mindfulness is the practice of being fully present and engaged in the present moment, with a non-judgmental awareness of one's thoughts, feelings, and sensations. By cultivating mindfulness, individuals can develop greater clarity, focus, and emotional resilience, enabling them to navigate life's challenges with grace and equanimity. Mindfulness practices such as meditation, deep breathing, and body scanning help individuals cultivate a sense of inner peace and balance, reduce stress and anxiety, and enhance overall well-being.

Self-Reflection: Self-reflection is the process of examining one's thoughts, feelings, and behaviors with honesty and curiosity, in order to gain insight into oneself and one's life experiences. By engaging in regular self-reflection, individuals can deepen their self-awareness, identify patterns and themes in their thoughts and behaviors, and gain clarity on their values, goals, and priorities. Self-reflection practices such as journaling, introspection, and mindfulness-based inquiry help individuals cultivate a deeper understanding of themselves, their relationships, and their life path, and empower them to make conscious choices that align with their authentic selves.

Continuous Learning: Continuous learning is the practice of seeking out new knowledge, skills, and experiences throughout one's life, in order to grow and evolve as a person. By committing to lifelong learning, individuals can expand their horizons, stay curious and engaged, and adapt to the ever-changing demands of the world around them. Continuous learning can take many forms, including formal education, self-study, mentorship, and experiential learning. Whether learning a new language, mastering a musical instrument, or acquiring a new professional skill, continuous learning opens doors to new opportunities, enriches one's life, and enhances personal and professional fulfillment.

In summary, mindfulness, self-reflection, and continuous learning are essential practices for cultivating personal excellence and living a life of purpose, passion, and fulfillment. By incorporating these practices into their daily lives, individuals can deepen their self-awareness, expand their knowledge and skills, and unlock their full potential, empowering them to create the life they desire and deserve.

# Chapter: Actionable Tips for Daily Habits that Enhance Well-Being and Fulfillment

Incorporating mindfulness, self-reflection, and continuous learning into our daily routines is key to fostering personal growth, enhancing well-being, and cultivating a sense of fulfillment. In this chapter, we offer actionable tips for integrating these habits into daily life, empowering individuals to thrive in all aspects of their lives.

Start Your Day Mindfully: Begin each day with a moment of mindfulness to set a positive tone for the day ahead. Upon waking, take a few deep breaths and center yourself in the present moment. Consider starting a morning ritual such as meditation, yoga, or a mindful walk to ground yourself and cultivate a sense of calm and clarity before diving into your day.

Schedule Regular Self-Reflection Time: Set aside dedicated time each day for self-reflection and introspection. This could be in the form of journaling, meditation, or simply quiet contemplation. Use this time to reflect on your thoughts, feelings, and experiences, and gain insight into your values, goals, and priorities. Consider keeping a gratitude journal to focus on the positive aspects of your life and cultivate an attitude of appreciation and abundance.

Embrace Lifelong Learning: Make learning a lifelong habit by incorporating it into your daily routine. Set aside time each day for reading, listening to podcasts, or engaging in online courses or workshops. Choose topics that interest you and align with your personal and professional goals, and commit to expanding your knowledge and skills on a regular basis. Take advantage of downtime, such as during your commute or while exercising, to consume educational content and feed your curiosity.

Practice Mindful Eating: Cultivate mindfulness in your eating habits by paying attention to the sensory experience of eating. Slow down and savor each bite, noticing the flavors, textures, and sensations of the food. Eat without distractions, such as television or screens, and listen to your body's hunger and fullness cues. By practicing mindful eating, you can develop a healthier relationship with food, increase enjoyment and satisfaction, and support overall well-being.

Prioritize Self-Care: Make self-care a non-negotiable part of your daily routine by scheduling time for activities that nourish your body, mind, and soul. Whether it's taking a relaxing bath, going for a nature walk, or practicing a hobby you enjoy, prioritize activities that recharge and rejuvenate you. Set boundaries around your time and energy, and honor your needs by saying no to activities or commitments that drain you or cause unnecessary stress.

Cultivate Gratitude and Positivity: Foster a habit of gratitude by incorporating daily practices that focus on appreciation and positivity. Start or end each day by reflecting on three things you're grateful for, no matter how small. Keep a gratitude journal to record your blessings and reflect on the positive aspects of your life. Surround yourself with positive influences, such as uplifting music, inspiring books, or supportive friends and family members, to cultivate a positive mindset and outlook on life.

By incorporating these actionable tips into your daily routine, you can cultivate habits of mindfulness, self-reflection, and continuous learning that enhance your overall well-being and fulfillment. Commit to making these habits a priority in your life, and watch as they transform your mindset, habits, and ultimately, your life for the better.

# Chapter: The Habits of Highly Effective Managers and Leaders

In the dynamic and ever-evolving landscape of business, effective management and leadership are essential for driving organizational success, fostering employee engagement, and achieving strategic objectives. In this chapter, we examine the habits of highly effective managers and leaders, exploring the key behaviors and practices that distinguish them and enable them to excel in their roles.

Clear Communication: Effective managers and leaders prioritize clear and transparent communication as a foundational habit. They communicate vision, goals, and expectations clearly and consistently, ensuring alignment and understanding across all levels of the organization. They are also active listeners, soliciting feedback, and fostering open dialogue to create a culture of trust, collaboration, and accountability.

Empowering and Developing Others: Highly effective managers and leaders empower their teams to take ownership of their work, make decisions, and contribute to the organization's success. They delegate tasks and responsibilities effectively, providing guidance and support as needed while allowing individuals to develop and grow in their roles. They invest in the development of their team members through coaching, mentorship, and training, fostering a culture of continuous learning and improvement.

Leading by Example: Effective managers and leaders lead by example, modeling the behaviors and values they expect from their team members. They demonstrate integrity, professionalism, and resilience in their actions and decisions, inspiring trust and confidence among their peers and subordinates. They uphold high standards of performance and behavior and hold themselves accountable for their actions, setting a positive example for others to follow.

Adaptability and Resilience: In today's fast-paced and uncertain business environment, effective managers and leaders are adaptable and resilient in the face of change and adversity. They embrace change as an opportunity for growth and innovation, remaining flexible and open-minded in their approach to problem-solving and decision-making. They remain calm and composed under pressure, inspiring confidence and stability in their teams and navigating challenges with confidence and grace.

Strategic Thinking and Decision-Making: Highly effective managers and leaders possess strong strategic thinking skills, enabling them to envision the future, anticipate opportunities and threats, and develop actionable plans to achieve organizational goals. They make informed decisions based on data, analysis, and sound judgment, weighing risks and benefits carefully and considering the long-term implications of their actions. They are also adept at prioritizing tasks and resources effectively, ensuring that efforts are aligned with strategic priorities and objectives.

Building and Nurturing Relationships: Effective managers and leaders recognize the importance of building and nurturing positive relationships with their team members, peers, and stakeholders. They foster a culture of trust, respect, and collaboration, valuing diversity of thought and perspective. They invest time and effort in building rapport and connections with others, actively seeking to understand their needs, motivations, and aspirations. They also cultivate a network of mentors, advisors, and allies who can provide support, guidance, and feedback to help them succeed in their roles.

In summary, the habits of highly effective managers and leaders encompass clear communication, empowering and developing others, leading by example, adaptability and resilience, strategic thinking, and decision-making, and building and nurturing relationships. By cultivating these habits, managers and leaders can inspire and motivate their teams, drive organizational success, and create a culture of excellence and innovation that propels the organization forward.

# Chapter: The Crucial Trio: Communication, Delegation, and Decision-Making in Leadership

Effective leadership is not just about charisma or vision—it's about mastering the art of communication, delegation, and decision-making. In this chapter, we delve into the pivotal role that these three elements play in shaping the success of leaders and organizations alike.

Communication: At the heart of effective leadership lies clear, transparent, and empathetic communication. Leaders must be able to articulate their vision, goals, and expectations with clarity, ensuring alignment and understanding across all levels of the organization. They must also be active listeners, soliciting feedback, and fostering open dialogue to create a culture of trust, collaboration, and accountability. Effective communication builds rapport, inspires confidence, and cultivates a sense of belonging among team members, empowering them to contribute their ideas, talents, and perspectives to the collective success of the organization.

Delegation: Effective leaders understand that they cannot do it all alone—they must empower their teams to take ownership of their work, make decisions, and contribute to the organization's success. Delegation is not just about assigning tasks; it's about entrusting individuals with responsibilities and authority, providing guidance and support as needed, and creating opportunities for growth and development. By delegating effectively, leaders free up their time and energy to focus on strategic priorities and high-impact initiatives, while also empowering their teams to learn, grow, and excel in their roles.

Decision-Making: Leaders are faced with countless decisions every day, ranging from routine tasks to complex strategic initiatives. Effective decision-making requires a blend of analysis, intuition, and sound judgment, as well as the ability to weigh risks and benefits, consider multiple perspectives, and anticipate potential outcomes. Leaders must be decisive yet adaptable, able to make timely decisions with confidence and conviction, while also remaining open to feedback and willing to course-correct as needed. By making informed and strategic decisions, leaders can steer the organization towards its goals, navigate challenges with resilience, and capitalize on opportunities for growth and innovation.

In summary, communication, delegation, and decision-making are the cornerstones of effective leadership, enabling leaders to inspire, motivate, and empower their teams to achieve extraordinary results. By mastering these essential skills and practices, leaders can create a culture of trust, collaboration, and accountability that fosters innovation, resilience, and sustained success for the organization and its members alike.

# Chapter: Case Studies of Successful Leaders Demonstrating Effective Communication, Delegation, and Decision-Making

In this chapter, we examine real-life examples of successful leaders who have demonstrated exemplary practices in communication, delegation, and decision-making, showcasing how these habits contribute to their success and the success of their organizations.

Indra Nooyi (Former CEO of PepsiCo): Indra Nooyi is widely regarded as one of the most influential and successful leaders in the business world, known for her strategic vision, effective communication skills, and inclusive leadership style. Throughout her tenure as CEO of PepsiCo, Nooyi emphasized the importance of clear and transparent communication, regularly engaging with employees, shareholders, and stakeholders to articulate the company's vision, values, and strategic priorities. She also demonstrated a strong commitment to delegation, empowering her team to take ownership of their work, make decisions, and drive innovation within the organization. Additionally, Nooyi's decisive and forward-thinking approach to decision-making enabled PepsiCo to navigate through challenging market conditions and capitalize on emerging opportunities, positioning the company for long-term growth and success.

Jeff Bezos (Founder and Former CEO of Amazon): Jeff Bezos is renowned for his visionary leadership and relentless focus on innovation, customer obsession, and long-term thinking. Throughout his tenure at Amazon, Bezos prioritized effective communication, ensuring that the company's goals, values, and customer-centric philosophy were clearly communicated and understood by employees at all levels of the organization. He also embraced delegation as a key leadership principle, empowering his team to experiment, take risks, and innovate on behalf of customers. Bezos' bold and data-driven approach to decision-making enabled Amazon to disrupt traditional industries, pioneer new technologies, and revolutionize the way people shop and consume goods and services around the world.

Mary Barra (CEO of General Motors): Mary Barra has earned widespread acclaim for her leadership at General Motors, where she has championed a culture of transparency, accountability, and collaboration. Barra's commitment to effective communication is evident in her regular town hall meetings, where she engages with employees to solicit feedback, address concerns, and reinforce the company's vision and values. She has also embraced delegation as a means of empowering her team to drive innovation and performance across the organization. Under Barra's leadership, General Motors has made strategic decisions to invest in electric and autonomous vehicles, positioning the company for success in the rapidly evolving automotive industry.

These case studies demonstrate how effective communication, delegation, and decision-making are essential traits of successful leaders. By embodying these habits in their leadership practices, Indra Nooyi, Jeff Bezos, Mary Barra, and other exemplary leaders have inspired their teams, driven organizational performance, and achieved remarkable success in their respective industries.

# Chapter: Unleashing the Power of Motivation and Inspiration

Motivation is the driving force behind our actions, fueling our pursuit of goals and aspirations. In this chapter, we delve into the psychology of motivation, exploring how habits influence motivation levels and examining strategies for fostering motivation and inspiration in our lives.

Understanding Motivation: Motivation is a complex psychological construct influenced by a myriad of factors, including our intrinsic desires, extrinsic rewards, and environmental cues. At its core, motivation is fueled by a combination of internal drives, such as the desire for mastery, autonomy, and purpose, and external incentives, such as recognition, rewards, and social approval. By understanding the underlying drivers of motivation, we can harness its power to propel us towards our goals and aspirations.

The Role of Habits: Habits play a critical role in shaping our motivation levels, as they influence our thoughts, feelings, and behaviors on a subconscious level. Positive habits, such as regular exercise, healthy eating, and goal-setting, can boost our motivation by providing structure, routine, and a sense of progress towards our goals. Conversely, negative habits, such as procrastination, self-doubt, and negative self-talk, can undermine our motivation and hinder our ability to achieve success.

Building Motivating Habits: To cultivate motivation and inspiration in our lives, it is essential to cultivate positive habits that support our goals and aspirations. This includes habits such as setting clear and achievable goals, breaking tasks into manageable steps, and celebrating progress and milestones along the way. By establishing routines and rituals that reinforce our commitment to our goals, we can create an environment that fosters motivation and propels us towards success.

Harnessing Intrinsic Motivation: Intrinsic motivation, or the desire to engage in an activity for its own sake, is a powerful driver of behavior and can sustain our motivation over the long term. To harness intrinsic motivation, it is essential to align our goals and activities with our values, interests, and passions. By pursuing activities that are personally meaningful and fulfilling, we can tap into a deep reservoir of motivation and inspiration that energizes us and propels us towards our goals.

Cultivating a Growth Mindset: A growth mindset, characterized by a belief in one's ability to learn and grow, is essential for maintaining motivation and resilience in the face of challenges and setbacks. By reframing failure as an opportunity for learning and growth, we can maintain a positive outlook and persevere in the pursuit of our goals. Cultivating a growth mindset involves challenging self-limiting beliefs, embracing challenges, and seeking out opportunities for learning and development.

In summary, motivation and inspiration are essential ingredients for success in any endeavor. By understanding the psychology of motivation and harnessing the power of habits, we can cultivate a mindset that propels us towards our goals, fosters resilience in the face of challenges, and enables us to live a life of purpose, passion, and fulfillment.

# Chapter: Strategies for Sustaining Motivation and Overcoming Obstacles

Embarking on the journey towards success is often accompanied by challenges, setbacks, and moments of doubt. In this chapter, we explore practical strategies for staying motivated and overcoming obstacles on the path to achieving our goals.

Define Your Why: Start by clarifying your reasons for pursuing your goals — the deeper meaning behind your aspirations. Reflect on what inspires and motivates you, and identify the values, passions, and desires that drive your actions. By connecting with your intrinsic motivations and understanding the significance of your goals, you can cultivate a sense of purpose and commitment that sustains you through challenges and setbacks.

Set Clear and Achievable Goals: Break down your long-term goals into smaller, manageable steps, and set clear, specific, and achievable milestones along the way. Create a roadmap that outlines the actions you need to take to progress towards your goals, and track your progress regularly. Celebrate your achievements and milestones, no matter how small, to maintain momentum and reinforce your sense of progress and accomplishment.

Cultivate a Growth Mindset: Embrace challenges, setbacks, and failures as opportunities for learning and growth. Adopt a growth mindset—a belief in your ability to learn, adapt, and improve over time—and view obstacles as temporary setbacks rather than insurmountable barriers. Focus on the lessons you can glean from adversity, and use them to inform your future actions and decisions.

Develop Resilience: Cultivate resilience—the ability to bounce back from setbacks and persevere in the face of adversity. Build a support network of friends, family, mentors, and peers who can provide encouragement, guidance, and perspective during challenging times. Practice self-care and stress management techniques, such as mindfulness, exercise, and relaxation exercises, to recharge and replenish your energy reserves.

Stay Focused on the Process: Shift your focus from outcomes to the process of working towards your goals. Instead of fixating on the end result, immerse yourself in the journey—the daily habits, actions, and behaviors that move you closer to your goals. Stay present and engaged in the present moment, and trust that consistent effort and perseverance will ultimately lead to success.

Stay Flexible and Adapt: Remain flexible and adaptable in the face of changing circumstances and unexpected obstacles. Be willing to adjust your plans, strategies, and timelines as needed, and view detours and setbacks as opportunities for growth and innovation. Maintain an open mind and a willingness to experiment, iterate, and course-correct along the way.

Visualize Success: Use visualization techniques to mentally rehearse your success and envision yourself achieving your goals. Create vivid, detailed mental images of your desired outcomes, and immerse yourself in the emotions and sensations of success. Visualization can help you maintain motivation, build confidence, and reinforce your belief in your ability to achieve your goals.

In conclusion, staying motivated and overcoming obstacles on the path to success requires a combination of clarity, resilience, adaptability, and focus. By defining your why, setting clear goals, cultivating a growth mindset, developing resilience, staying focused on the process, staying flexible and adaptable, and visualizing success, you can navigate challenges and setbacks with confidence and determination, and ultimately achieve your goals.

# Chapter: The Transformative Power of Positive Thinking and Motivated Habits

Positive thinking is not just a fleeting mindset—it is a powerful tool that can shape our attitudes, behaviors, and our outcomes in life. In this chapter, we explore how positive thinking, coupled with motivated habits, can create a mindset that fosters resilience, motivation, and success.

The Power of Positive Thinking: Positive thinking is the practice of maintaining a constructive and optimistic outlook on life, even in the face of challenges and setbacks. By focusing on the potential for growth, learning, and opportunity in every situation, positive thinkers cultivate a mindset that is conducive to resilience, creativity, and problem-solving. Positive thinking has been linked to numerous psychological and physiological benefits, including reduced stress, improved mood, enhanced immune function, and greater overall well-being.

Cultivating Positive Habits: Habits are the building blocks of our daily routines and behaviors, shaping our thoughts, feelings, and actions on a subconscious level. By cultivating positive habits that reinforce optimistic thinking and motivated behavior, we can create a virtuous cycle that sustains our motivation and propels us towards our goals. Examples of positive habits that promote a motivated mindset include daily affirmations, visualization exercises, gratitude journaling, and regular exercise.

Rewiring the Brain: The brain is highly adaptable and capable of forming new neural connections in response to our experiences and behaviors—a phenomenon known as neuroplasticity. By consistently practicing positive thinking and motivated habits, we can literally rewire our brains to become more resilient, optimistic, and motivated over time. This rewiring process strengthens the neural pathways associated with positive emotions and behaviors, making it easier for us to maintain a motivated mindset in the face of challenges and setbacks.

Overcoming Negative Self-Talk: Negative self-talk—the inner dialogue of self-criticism, doubt, and pessimism—can sabotage our motivation and confidence, preventing us from reaching our full potential. By cultivating awareness of our thought patterns and challenging negative self-talk with positive affirmations and reframing techniques, we can break free from self-limiting beliefs and cultivate a more empowered and optimistic mindset. Positive affirmations, visualization exercises, and mindfulness practices can help us cultivate self-compassion, self-confidence, and self-belief, empowering us to overcome obstacles and achieve our goals.

Surrounding Yourself with Positivity: Our environment plays a significant role in shaping our thoughts, emotions, and behaviors. Surrounding ourselves with positive influences—such as supportive friends, uplifting music, inspiring books, and motivating quotes—can reinforce our commitment to positive thinking and motivated habits, creating an environment that nurtures our growth and success. Likewise, minimizing exposure to negative influences—such as toxic relationships, pessimistic media, and self-doubt—can protect our mindset and preserve our motivation.

In summary, positive thinking and motivated habits are powerful tools for cultivating a mindset that fosters resilience, motivation, and success. By consciously practicing positive thinking, cultivating positive habits, rewiring our brains, overcoming negative self-talk, and surrounding ourselves with positivity, we can create a mindset that empowers us to overcome obstacles, achieve our goals, and live a life of purpose, passion, and fulfillment.

# Chapter: Mastering Personal Finance: Habits for Financial Success and Stability

Achieving financial success and stability requires more than just luck—it requires deliberate habits and practices that promote smart money management, discipline, and long-term planning. In this chapter, we explore the essential habits and practices necessary for mastering personal finance and building a solid foundation for financial well-being.

Budgeting and Expense Tracking: Budgeting is the cornerstone of effective money management, allowing individuals to track their income and expenses, prioritize spending, and allocate resources towards their financial goals. Start by creating a detailed budget that outlines your monthly income, fixed expenses (such as rent/mortgage, utilities, and loan payments), variable expenses (such as groceries, entertainment, and transportation), and savings goals. Track your expenses regularly and adjust your budget as needed to ensure that you're living within your means and making progress towards your financial objectives.

Saving and Investing: Saving and investing are crucial habits for building wealth and achieving financial security over the long term. Aim to save a portion of your income each month—ideally, at least 20%—and allocate it towards an emergency fund, retirement savings, and other financial goals. Consider automating your savings by setting up automatic transfers from your checking account to your savings or investment accounts. Additionally, explore investment opportunities such as stocks, bonds, mutual funds, and retirement accounts (such as 401(k)s and IRAs) to grow your wealth and secure your financial future.

Debt Management: Managing debt is a critical aspect of personal finance, as excessive debt can hinder your ability to achieve financial goals and build wealth. Develop a strategy for paying off high-interest debt—such as credit card debt and personal loans—as quickly as possible, prioritizing debts with the highest interest rates first. Consider consolidating or refinancing your debts to secure lower interest rates and reduce your monthly payments. Avoid taking on new debt whenever possible and focus on living within your means to prevent future financial strain.

Financial Education and Literacy: Educating yourself about personal finance is essential for making informed decisions and navigating the complexities of the financial world. Take advantage of resources such as books, podcasts, online courses, and workshops to improve your financial literacy and gain a deeper understanding of topics such as budgeting, investing, retirement planning, and tax management. Additionally, seek advice from financial professionals, such as certified financial planners (CFPs) or investment advisors, to develop personalized strategies that align with your goals and values.

Long-Term Planning: Successful financial management requires a long-term perspective and strategic planning for the future. Set clear, achievable financial goals for yourself — whether it's buying a home, saving for your children's education, or retiring comfortably — and develop a roadmap for achieving them. Consider factors such as your age, income, expenses, risk tolerance, and time horizon when crafting your financial plan, and revisit it regularly to track your progress and make adjustments as needed.

Practicing Discipline and Delayed Gratification: Finally, mastering personal finance requires discipline and the ability to delay gratification in favor of long-term financial security. Practice self-control when it comes to spending and avoid impulsive purchases that may derail your financial goals. Instead, focus on making intentional spending decisions that align with your values and priorities, and remind yourself of the bigger picture whenever temptation strikes.

In summary, mastering personal finance requires a combination of smart money habits, disciplined spending, and strategic planning. By budgeting effectively, saving and investing wisely, managing debt responsibly, educating yourself about financial matters, setting clear goals, and practicing discipline and delayed gratification, you can build a solid foundation for financial success and stability, and achieve your long-term financial aspirations.

# Chapter: Building Financial Wellness: Budgeting, Saving, Investing, and Debt Management

Financial wellness is a journey that begins with mastering the fundamental principles of budgeting, saving, investing, and debt management. In this chapter, we explore these essential topics and provide practical strategies for achieving financial stability and success.

Budgeting: Budgeting is the cornerstone of effective financial management, providing a roadmap for how you allocate your income towards expenses, savings, and investments. Start by tracking your monthly income and expenses, categorizing your spending into fixed expenses (e.g., rent, utilities) and variable expenses (e.g., groceries, entertainment). Identify areas where you can cut back on discretionary spending and allocate those savings towards your financial goals. Regularly review and adjust your budget to ensure that it aligns with your priorities and helps you achieve your objectives.

Saving: Saving is the foundation of building wealth and achieving financial security over the long term. Aim to save a portion of your income each month, ideally at least 20% or more. Establish an emergency fund to cover unexpected expenses, such as medical bills or car repairs, with three to six months' worth of living expenses. Additionally, set aside savings for short-term goals (e.g., vacations, home renovations) and long-term goals (e.g., retirement, children's education). Consider automating your savings by setting up automatic transfers from your checking account to your savings account to ensure consistency and discipline.

Investing: Investing is essential for growing your wealth and achieving your long-term financial goals. Start by educating yourself about different investment options, such as stocks, bonds, mutual funds, and exchange-traded funds (ETFs). Consider factors such as risk tolerance, investment time horizon, and financial goals when designing your investment portfolio. Diversify your investments across different asset classes to reduce risk and maximize returns. Regularly review and rebalance your portfolio to ensure that it remains aligned with your investment objectives and risk tolerance.

Debt Management: Managing debt is crucial for maintaining financial health and stability. Start by assessing your current debt situation, including outstanding balances, interest rates, and minimum monthly payments. Develop a strategy for paying off high-interest debt, such as credit card debt or personal loans, by prioritizing debts with the highest interest rates first. Consider consolidating or refinancing your debt to secure lower interest rates and reduce your overall monthly payments. Avoid taking on new debt whenever possible and focus on living within your means to prevent future financial strain.

In summary, mastering budgeting, saving, investing, and debt management is essential for achieving financial wellness and building a solid foundation for future success. By practicing disciplined financial habits, setting clear financial goals, and making informed financial decisions, you can take control of your finances and create a brighter financial future for yourself and your family.

# Chapter: Practical Steps for Developing Healthy Financial Habits and Achieving Long-Term Goals

Achieving long-term financial success requires more than just good intentions — it requires deliberate action and consistent habits that support your financial goals. In this chapter, we provide practical advice for developing healthy financial habits and setting yourself up for long-term financial success.

Establish Clear Financial Goals: Start by defining your financial goals — both short-term and long-term. Whether it's buying a home, saving for retirement, paying off debt, or building an emergency fund, having clear goals gives you a sense of purpose and direction. Make sure your goals are specific, measurable, achievable, relevant, and time-bound (SMART), and prioritize them based on their importance and urgency.

Create a Realistic Budget: Develop a budget that aligns with your financial goals and lifestyle. Start by tracking your income and expenses to understand where your money is going each month. Then, allocate your income towards essential expenses (e.g., housing, utilities, groceries), savings, debt repayment, and discretionary spending. Be realistic about your expenses and make adjustments as needed to ensure that you're living within your means.

Automate Your Finances: Take advantage of technology to automate your finances and make managing your money easier and more efficient. Set up automatic transfers from your checking account to your savings or investment accounts to ensure that you're consistently saving and investing towards your goals. Consider automating bill payments and debt repayments to avoid late fees and penalties. By automating your finances, you can streamline your money management and reduce the risk of overspending or forgetting to save.

Prioritize Saving and Investing: Make saving and investing a priority in your financial plan. Aim to save a portion of your income each month, ideally at least 20% or more. Start by building an emergency fund to cover unexpected expenses, with three to six months' worth of living expenses. Then, focus on long-term investments, such as retirement accounts (e.g., 401(k), IRA) and taxable investment accounts, to grow your wealth over time. Consider enrolling in employer-sponsored retirement plans and taking advantage of employer matching contributions, if available.

Manage Debt Wisely: Develop a strategy for managing and paying off debt effectively. Start by prioritizing high-interest debt, such as credit card debt or personal loans, and making extra payments towards those balances to reduce interest costs. Consider consolidating or refinancing your debt to secure lower interest rates and reduce your monthly payments. Avoid taking on new debt whenever possible and focus on living within your means to prevent future financial strain.

Educate Yourself About Personal Finance: Take the time to educate yourself about personal finance and investing. There are plenty of resources available, including books, podcasts, online courses, and workshops, that can help you improve your financial literacy and make informed financial decisions. Stay up-to-date on financial news and trends, and seek advice from trusted financial professionals, such as certified financial planners (CFPs) or investment advisors, when needed.

Stay Flexible and Adapt: Life is unpredictable, and your financial situation may change over time. Stay flexible and adaptable in your approach to managing your finances, and be willing to adjust your goals and strategies as needed. Keep an open mind and be proactive about finding solutions to challenges or setbacks that may arise along the way. By staying flexible and adapting to changing circumstances, you can navigate the ups and downs of life with confidence and resilience.

In summary, developing healthy financial habits and achieving long-term financial goals requires discipline, consistency, and perseverance. By establishing clear goals, creating a realistic budget, automating your finances, prioritizing saving, and investing, managing debt wisely, educating yourself about personal finance, and staying flexible and adaptable, you can set yourself up for long-term financial success and build a brighter financial future for yourself and your family.

# Chapter: Streamlining Processes and Infrastructure: Enhancing Efficiency in Business and Life

In both business and personal endeavors, efficiency and optimization are crucial for maximizing productivity, minimizing waste, and achieving desired outcomes. In this chapter, we delve into the importance of streamlining processes and infrastructure, exploring how efficiency can drive success in various aspects of life.

The Value of Efficiency: Efficiency refers to the ability to accomplish tasks or goals with minimal waste of time, resources, or effort. Whether in business operations or personal tasks, efficiency allows us to accomplish more in less time, freeing up resources for other priorities and activities. By streamlining processes and infrastructure, we can reduce bottlenecks, eliminate redundancies, and optimize workflows to achieve better results with greater ease.

Business Efficiency: In business, efficiency is essential for maximizing profitability, competitiveness, and customer satisfaction. Streamlining processes and infrastructure allows businesses to operate more smoothly and cost-effectively, enabling them to deliver products or services faster, cheaper, and with higher quality. From lean manufacturing principles to digital automation tools, businesses can leverage various strategies and technologies to enhance efficiency across all aspects of their operations, from production and logistics to marketing and customer service.

Personal Efficiency: Efficiency is equally important in personal life, where time and resources are often limited. By optimizing daily routines, habits, and workflows, individuals can accomplish more in less time and with less effort, freeing up time for leisure, self-care, and pursuing personal goals. From adopting time management techniques to decluttering physical and digital spaces, there are numerous ways to enhance personal efficiency and productivity.

Identifying and Eliminating Waste: One of the keys to efficiency is identifying and eliminating waste—any activity, process, or resource that does not add value to the end result. In business, waste can take many forms, such as excess inventory, unnecessary paperwork, or inefficient production processes. By conducting regular audits and assessments, businesses can identify areas of waste and implement strategies to reduce or eliminate them, thereby improving efficiency and profitability.

Embracing Technology and Innovation: Technology and innovation play a critical role in driving efficiency and optimization in both business and personal life. From advanced data analytics and artificial intelligence to smart devices and digital platforms, technology offers a myriad of tools and solutions for streamlining processes, automating repetitive tasks, and improving decision-making. By embracing technology and staying abreast of emerging trends and developments, businesses and individuals can stay competitive and achieve greater levels of efficiency and productivity.

Continuous Improvement: Efficiency is not a one-time achievement but an ongoing process of continuous improvement. By fostering a culture of innovation, collaboration, and learning, businesses and individuals can continually identify opportunities for optimization and refinement, striving for excellence in all that they do. From small incremental changes to larger transformative initiatives, every effort towards improvement contributes to greater efficiency and success in the long run.

In summary, streamlining processes and infrastructure is essential for enhancing efficiency and optimization in both business and personal life. By identifying areas of waste, embracing technology and innovation, and fostering a culture of continuous improvement, businesses and individuals can achieve greater levels of productivity, profitability, and satisfaction, ultimately realizing their full potential and achieving their goals.

# Chapter: Mastering Time Management, Organization, and Prioritization Habits

Time is a finite resource, and how we manage it can greatly impact our productivity, success, and overall well-being. In this chapter, we'll explore essential habits related to time management, organization, and prioritization that can help individuals optimize their use of time and achieve their goals effectively.

Time Management Habits:
Time management is the practice of planning and allocating time to tasks and activities in a way that maximizes productivity and minimizes wasted time. Here are some key time management habits to cultivate:

a. Prioritize Tasks: Identify your most important tasks and prioritize them based on urgency and importance. Use techniques like the Eisenhower Matrix to categorize tasks into four quadrants: urgent and important, important but not urgent, urgent but not important, and neither urgent nor important.

b. Set SMART Goals: Set specific, measurable, achievable, relevant, and time-bound (SMART) goals to provide clarity and direction for your efforts. Break down larger goals into smaller, actionable steps, and set deadlines to keep yourself accountable.

c. Plan Your Day: Take time at the beginning of each day to plan your schedule and prioritize your tasks. Use tools like to-do lists, calendars, and time-blocking techniques to allocate time for important tasks and avoid overcommitting yourself.

d. Minimize Distractions: Identify common distractions that may derail your focus and productivity, such as social media, email, or multitasking. Take steps to minimize or eliminate these distractions, such as turning off notifications, setting designated times for checking email, and creating a distraction-free work environment.

Organization Habits:
Organization is the key to maintaining clarity, efficiency, and peace of mind in both work and life. Here are some organization habits to adopt:

a. Declutter Regularly: Keep your physical and digital spaces organized by regularly decluttering and eliminating unnecessary items or files. Use systems such as the KonMari method for decluttering physical possessions and digital tools for organizing files and documents.

b. Create Systems and Processes: Develop systems and processes for managing tasks, information, and workflows efficiently. Use tools like project management software, file organization systems, and automation tools to streamline repetitive tasks and ensure consistency.

c. Maintain a Calendar: Use a calendar or scheduling tool to keep track of appointments, deadlines, and commitments. Color-code events and tasks, set reminders, and sync your calendar across devices to stay organized and on top of your schedule.

d. Practice the Two-Minute Rule: Adopt the two-minute rule, which states that if a task takes less than two minutes to complete, do it immediately. This helps prevent small tasks from piling up and becoming overwhelming.

Prioritization Habits:
Prioritization is the process of determining which tasks or activities are most important and deserving of your time and attention. Here are some prioritization habits to develop:

a. Use the 80/20 Rule: Apply the Pareto Principle, also known as the 80/20 rule, which suggests that 80% of results come from 20% of efforts. Identify the tasks or activities that yield the greatest impact or results and prioritize them accordingly.

b. Practice Ruthless Prioritization: Be selective about where you invest your time and energy, and focus on activities that align with your goals and values. Learn to say no to low-priority tasks or commitments that detract from your focus and productivity.

c. Reevaluate Priorities Regularly: Periodically reassess your priorities and adjust them as needed based on changing circumstances, goals, or priorities. Be flexible and willing to adapt your plans and commitments to stay aligned with your overarching objectives.

d. Delegate or Outsource: Recognize when tasks can be delegated to others or outsourced to external resources. Delegate tasks that are outside your area of expertise or require specialized skills, freeing up your time to focus on higher-value activities.

By cultivating these habits related to time management, organization, and prioritization, individuals can optimize their use of time, increase their productivity, and achieve their goals with greater efficiency and effectiveness.

# Chapter: Strategies for Streamlining Processes and Improving Infrastructure

In today's fast-paced world, efficiency and effectiveness are paramount for success in both business and personal endeavors. In this chapter, we'll explore practical strategies for streamlining processes and enhancing infrastructure to increase productivity and effectiveness.

Identify Bottlenecks and Inefficiencies: Start by conducting a thorough assessment of your current processes and infrastructure to identify bottlenecks, inefficiencies, and areas for improvement. Look for tasks or steps that are time-consuming, redundant, or prone to errors. Gather feedback from stakeholders, team members, and customers to gain insights into pain points and opportunities for optimization.

Standardize and Document Procedures: Develop standardized procedures and workflows for key processes to ensure consistency and efficiency. Document these procedures in a centralized repository, such as an operations manual or knowledge base, and make them easily accessible to relevant stakeholders. Provide training and support to ensure that team members understand and adhere to these standardized procedures.

Embrace Automation and Technology: Leverage automation tools and technology solutions to streamline repetitive tasks, eliminate manual errors, and improve overall efficiency. Explore software applications, such as project management tools, customer relationship management (CRM) systems, and workflow automation platforms, that can automate routine tasks and streamline communication, collaboration, and decision-making processes. Invest in technology infrastructure, such as cloud computing services and digital platforms, to enhance scalability, flexibility, and accessibility.

Implement Lean Principles: Apply lean principles and methodologies, such as Lean Six Sigma, to identify and eliminate waste in your processes. Focus on optimizing value-added activities while minimizing non-value-added activities, such as waiting, overproduction, or unnecessary transportation. Use tools like value stream mapping and root cause analysis to identify inefficiencies and develop targeted solutions for improvement.

Foster a Culture of Continuous Improvement: Cultivate a culture of continuous improvement and innovation within your organization or team. Encourage open communication, collaboration, and feedback-sharing among team members, and empower them to suggest and implement process improvements. Establish regular review cycles to assess progress, celebrate successes, and identify opportunities for further optimization. Recognize and reward individuals or teams who contribute to process improvement initiatives.

Prioritize Scalability and Flexibility: Design processes and infrastructure with scalability and flexibility in mind to accommodate growth, changes, and evolving needs over time. Consider factors such as future demand, technological advancements, and market trends when designing or updating processes and infrastructure. Invest in modular and scalable solutions that can adapt to changing requirements without significant disruption or rework.

Monitor Performance and KPIs: Establish key performance indicators (KPIs) and metrics to measure the effectiveness and efficiency of your processes and infrastructure. Track relevant metrics, such as cycle time, throughput, error rates, and customer satisfaction, to assess performance and identify areas for improvement. Use data analytics and reporting tools to analyze trends, identify root causes of issues, and make data-driven decisions for optimization.

By implementing these strategies for streamlining processes and improving infrastructure, organizations and individuals can increase productivity, reduce costs, and enhance overall effectiveness in achieving their goals and objectives. Continuous refinement and adaptation are essential for staying competitive and achieving sustainable success in today's dynamic and ever-changing environment.

# Conclusion: Cultivating Highly Effective Habits for Success

Throughout this book, we've explored the power of highly effective habits and their transformative impact on various aspects of life, from personal development to business success. As we conclude our journey, let's recap some key takeaways and reinforce the importance of cultivating these habits for lasting success.

Mindset Matters: Success starts with the right mindset. Cultivate a growth mindset that embraces challenges, seeks continuous improvement, and believes in your ability to learn and grow.

Clear Goals and Priorities: Define your goals and priorities clearly, both in business and personal life. Set SMART goals and align your actions with your values and aspirations.

Efficiency and Organization: Streamline your processes, improve infrastructure, and embrace technology to increase efficiency and productivity. Stay organized, prioritize tasks, and eliminate waste to make the most of your time and resources.

Financial Wellness: Master personal finance habits such as budgeting, saving, investing, and debt management. Build a solid financial foundation to achieve your long-term goals and secure your financial future.

Leadership and Communication: Develop effective leadership and communication skills to inspire and motivate others. Lead by example, communicate clearly and empathetically, and foster a culture of collaboration and innovation.

Continuous Improvement: Embrace a mindset of continuous improvement and lifelong learning. Stay curious, adapt to change, and seek opportunities for growth and development in every aspect of your life.

The Power of Habits: Finally, recognize the profound impact that habits have on our lives. By cultivating highly effective habits—whether it's time management, organization, prioritization, or resilience—we can unlock our full potential, overcome obstacles, and achieve our most ambitious goals.

In essence, success is not just about talent or luck—it's about the habits we cultivate and the actions we take consistently over time. By embracing highly effective habits and integrating them into our daily lives, we can create a roadmap to success and fulfillment that transcends boundaries and empowers us to live our best lives. So, let's commit to cultivating these habits, one step at a time, and embark on a journey of growth, achievement, and endless possibilities.

# Chapter: Take Action: Committing to Highly Effective Habits

As you've journeyed through the pages of this book, you've gained valuable insights into the power of highly effective habits and their profound impact on success, fulfillment, and overall well-being. Now, it is time to act and commit to integrating these habits into your life.

Reflect on Your Goals: Take a moment to reflect on your personal and professional goals. What do you aspire to achieve? What areas of your life do you want to improve? Clarify your goals and envision the future you desire.

Identify Key Habits: Identify the key habits that align with your goals and priorities. Whether it's time management, organization, financial discipline, or personal development, pinpoint the habits that will move you closer to your objectives.

Set Clear Intentions: Set clear intentions to integrate these habits into your daily routine. Write down your intentions, break them down into actionable steps, and create a plan for implementation.

Start Small: Begin by incorporating one or two new habits into your daily life. Start small and gradually build momentum over time. Focus on consistency rather than perfection, and celebrate small victories along the way.

Create Accountability: Share your goals and intentions with a trusted friend, mentor, or accountability partner. Accountability can help keep you motivated, accountable, and on track towards your goals.

Track Your Progress: Keep track of your progress and monitor your adherence to your new habits. Use tools such as habit trackers, journals, or apps to monitor your daily activities and measure your progress over time.

Stay Resilient: Understand that building new habits takes time and effort. Be patient with yourself, and embrace setbacks as opportunities for growth and learning. Stay resilient, persevere through challenges, and keep moving forward towards your goals.

Celebrate Success: Celebrate your successes and milestones along the way. Acknowledge your progress, no matter how small, and take pride in your accomplishments. Celebrating success reinforces positive behaviors and motivates you to continue your journey towards success.

Review and Adjust: Regularly review your habits and progress, and be willing to adjust your approach as needed. Stay open to feedback, learn from your experiences, and continuously refine your habits to better align with your goals and values.

Embrace the Journey: Finally, embrace the journey of personal growth and self-discovery. Cultivating highly effective habits is not just about achieving specific outcomes—it's about becoming the best version of yourself and living a life of purpose, passion, and fulfillment.

In conclusion, committing to integrating highly effective habits into your life is a powerful investment in your future success and well-being. By taking action, staying resilient, and embracing the journey, you can unlock your full potential and create the life you've always dreamed of. So, seize this opportunity, and embark on a transformative journey towards a brighter, more fulfilling future.

# Chapter: Transformative Change: Achieving Lasting Success through Effective Habits

The adoption and sustenance of highly effective habits have the power to catalyze transformative change in our lives, leading to lasting success, fulfillment, and personal growth. In this chapter, we delve into the profound impact that these habits can have on our journey towards realizing our full potential.

Unlocking Potential: Effective habits act as catalysts for unlocking our untapped potential and propelling us towards our goals. By cultivating habits such as goal-setting, time management, and continuous learning, we tap into reservoirs of talent, creativity, and resilience that enable us to surpass our perceived limitations and achieve remarkable feats.

Creating Momentum: Adopting highly effective habits creates a ripple effect that generates momentum and propels us forward on our path to success. As we consistently practice these habits, we build momentum, overcome obstacles, and gain traction towards our goals, fueling our progress and reinforcing positive behaviors along the way.

Building Resilience: Effective habits serve as pillars of resilience, fortifying our mental, emotional, and physical well-being in the face of adversity. By cultivating habits such as mindfulness, self-care, and adaptive thinking, we develop the resilience to navigate life's challenges with grace, perseverance, and optimism, emerging stronger and more resilient with each trial we overcome.

Sustaining Success: The adoption and sustenance of highly effective habits are not merely means to an end but lifelong practices that underpin sustained success and fulfillment. By embedding these habits into our daily routines and lifestyles, we create a solid foundation for long-term success, resilience, and well-being, ensuring that our achievements endure and flourish over time.

Cultivating Excellence: Effective habits are the cornerstone of excellence, enabling us to consistently perform at our best and strive for greatness in all areas of our lives. Whether in our careers, relationships, health, or personal development, these habits foster a culture of excellence that propels us towards the highest levels of achievement and fulfillment.

Inspiring Others: As we embody and exemplify highly effective habits in our lives, we become beacons of inspiration and catalysts for change, inspiring others to follow suit and embark on their own journey of personal growth and transformation. Our actions speak volumes, and by modeling the power of effective habits, we empower others to unleash their potential and pursue their dreams with passion and purpose.

In conclusion, the adoption and sustenance of highly effective habits hold the key to transformative change and lasting success in our lives. By embracing these habits, we unlock our potential, create momentum, build resilience, sustain success, cultivate excellence, and inspire others to join us on the path to greatness. So, let us commit to integrating these habits into our lives and embark on a journey of transformation, growth, and fulfillment that knows no bounds.

www.ingramcontent.com/pod-product-compliance
Lightning Source LLC
Chambersburg PA
CBHW070406230526
45471CB00006B/2686